World of Islam

Islam in America

MASON CREST PUBLISHERS
PHILADELPHIA

World of Islam

World of Islam

Islam in America

ANNA MELMAN

Editorial Consultants: Foreign Policy Research Institute, Philadelphia, PA

Mason Crest Publishers
370 Reed Road
Broomall, PA 19008
www.masoncrest.com

First printing

1 3 5 7 9 8 6 4 2

Library of Congress Cataloging-in-Publication Data

Melman, Anna.
  Islam in America / Anna Melman.
     p. cm. — (World of Islam)
  ISBN 978-1-4222-0535-8 (hardcover) — ISBN 978-1-4222-0802-1 (pbk.)
  1. Muslims—United States—Juvenile literature. 2. Islam—United States—Juvenile literature. I. Title.
  BP67.A1M45 2006
  297.0973—dc22
                              2008053416

Photo Credits: 7: Katrina Thomas/Saudi Aramco World/Padia; 9: Library of Congress; 10: Library of Congress; 11: Library of Congress; 12: Library of Congress; 13: (inset) Used under license from Shutterstock, Inc.; Image courtesy Namallom (http://tebyan.net); 16: Katrina Thomas/Saudi Aramco World/Padia; 18: © OTTN Publishing, LLC; 19: Used under license from Shutterstock, Inc.; 21: Anne B. Hood; 23: William Tracy/Saudi Aramco World/Padia; 24: Used under license from Shutterstock, Inc.; 27: Jaap Steinvoorte (www.flickr.com/photos/stoneford/2489056249); 28: Used under license from Shutterstock, Inc.; 29: Used under license from Shutterstock, Inc.; 30: Used under license from Shutterstock, Inc.; 32: Soman; 33: Casey Lehman; 35: UN Photo; 37: Soman; 38: UN Photo; 42: Petty Officer 1st Class Michael B. W. Watkins/U.S. Navy/DoD; 45: Jeremy Burgin; 46: Federal Bureau of Investigation; 47: Adrian Pingstone; 48: Department of Defense; 52: Library of Congress; 53: Cpl. Jose O. Mediavilla, USMC/DoD; 55: © OTTN Publishing, LLC; 57: Used under license from Shutterstock, Inc.

Anna Melman is deputy editor at the Global Research in International Affairs (GLORIA) Center. She is also assistant editor of the *Turkish Studies* journal and of the *Middle East Review of International Affairs (MERIA) Journal.*

Table of Contents

History of Muslims in America

Muslims make up only a small percentage of the U.S. population, but they are an integral part of the American mosaic. Muslims first arrived on the shores of what is now the United States five centuries ago, though their presence in, influence on, and integration into American life really began at the end of the 19th century. Today, Muslims as a community are more prominent in the United States than ever.

Estimates of the number of Muslims in the United States vary dramatically, from just over 1 million to nearly 7 million, depending on the particular polling organization, scholarly group, or other entity doing the estimating. The U.S. Census Bureau does not ask about religion, and thus there are no official statistics. The CIA World Factbook estimated the U.S. population in July 2009 at a little more than 307 million and the percentage of Muslims at 0.6 percent, which would mean that some

Muslims chat outside their mosque after Sunday prayers. Because the U.S. census does not record religious affiliation, the exact number of Americans who follow Islam is unknown. Estimates range from slightly more than 1 million to about 7 million.

1.84 million people in the United States are adherents of Islam. In any case, the Muslim population in the United States is on the rise because of natural growth, continued immigration of Muslims, and conversion to Islam.

Regardless of the exact number of believers, the Muslim community in the United States is ethnically, culturally, geographically, and religiously diverse. Most Muslims are well integrated and assimilated into American life, while a small yet influential percentage identify with radical Islamism. There are numerous Muslim organizations that serve the religious, cultural, social, and political needs and interests of the community. Since the terrorist attacks of September 11, 2001, Muslims in the United States have been in the spotlight. Their attitudes toward the country—as well as the attitudes of non-Muslim Americans toward followers of Islam—have received a great deal of attention.

The First Muslims in America

Some scholars believe that the first Muslims in the New World arrived with the Spanish explorers of the late 15th and early 16th century. In fact, certain scholars cite evidence that Muslims were among the crew members of Columbus's first voyage of discovery, in 1492—the same year that Muslim rule in Iberia ended and a prohibition on Islamic practice was enacted in Spain. Furthermore, these scholars believe that Muslims on the early voyages to the New World intermarried with indigenous people, citing as evidence artifacts, inscriptions, and linguistic similarities between native languages and Arabic. Nonetheless, there is no scholarly consensus on this theory of an early Muslim presence in the Americas.

Estevanico is often cited as the first Muslim to reach the land that is now the United States. The slave, born in Morocco around 1500, accompanied the expedition of Panfilo de Narváez, which

Christopher Columbus lands in the Western Hemisphere, claiming the territory for Spain. Some historians believe that when Columbus set sail in 1492, his crew included several Muslims.

landed in present-day Tampa Bay, Florida, in 1528. The expedition was a disaster: of the 300 men who went ashore in Florida, just 4—including Estevanico and Álvar Núñez de Cabeza de Vaca, who took command after the death of Narváez—survived. After being shipwrecked in Texas, they wandered across the American Southwest before staggering into Mexico City in 1536.

It is widely accepted that significant numbers of Muslims first arrived in North America during the 17th century, as a result of the slave trade. They came from West Africa. It is estimated that between 10 and 20 percent of African slaves were originally Muslim. However, in most cases, due to the nature of slavery, including the separation of children from their parents and the Christianization of slaves by their masters, Muslim religious practice was not passed on.

A 19th-century engraving depicting a group of slaves. A significant portion of the slaves brought from Africa to the Western Hemisphere—estimates range from 10 to 20 percent—were originally Muslims. Once in the New World, however, most eventually abandoned their Islamic practices.

Waves of Immigration

Voluntary immigration of Muslims to the United States occurred in several waves. The first began on a small-scale in the 1870s and lasted until World War I (1914–1918). The first Muslims to reach the United States during this period were Arabs from the Ottoman Empire, principally from the eastern Mediterranean region, as well as from Yemen. Christian Arabs had gone to the United States and returned wealthy. Muslims sought to do the same.

Most arrived in the United States without their wives and did menial labor such as mining, migrant work, and peddling, competing with other immigrants for jobs. Those Muslim women who did go to the United States tended to work in mills and factories.

Because of the economic hardships these immigrant Muslims faced, many of them were unable to return home and ended up settling in the United States permanently. The end of this period saw the immigration of Muslims from the Balkan Peninsula and Eastern Europe as well.

After World War I, Muslim immigration, particularly from the Middle East, continued as the Ottoman Empire crumbled. Most of these immigrants were relatives of people who had come earlier. However, U.S. immigration laws passed in 1921 and 1924 imposed quotas on the number of immigrants that would be accepted into the country based on national origins. These laws had the effect of significantly restricting the number of immigrants from countries with large Muslim populations. Throughout the 1930s, almost all of the Muslims who were able to immigrate were related to people already settled in the United States.

This political cartoon from 1921 depicts Uncle Sam allowing only a trickle of immigrants to come to U.S. shores. Immigration laws passed in 1921 and 1924, which imposed quotas based on national origins, had the effect of preventing Muslims from entering the United States.

After World War II (1939–1945), Muslim immigration rose again, with war refugees arriving from Eastern Europe (mainly the Balkans), and later from the Middle East, the Indian Subcontinent, and the Soviet Union. The Nationality Act of 1953 still placed a quota on immigrants from each country based on populations in the United States at the end of the 19th century, which meant that Muslim immigration was still restricted.

Most of the post–World War II Muslim immigrants to the United States settled in urban centers, especially Chicago and New York. Many of these immigrants were well educated and from urban environments. Some were members of elite families. This meant that they often had Western attitudes and wished to pursue education or technical training. Beginning in the 1950s, it was easier for students to come to the United States to pursue advanced degrees, something many Muslims did.

The largest wave of Muslim immigration to the United States began in the 1960s. It was spurred by both the liberalization of U.S. immigration policy and events occurring across areas where Muslims lived. In 1965, President Lyndon B. Johnson signed an act repealing the quota system based on national origin. The percentage of immigrants from Europe declined, while the proportion from the Middle East and Asia increased. More than half of the new immigrants from these places were Muslim.

President Lyndon B. Johnson. Johnson signed into law the Immigration Act of 1965, which eliminated the national-origins quota system. This ultimately led to a rise in the number of Muslim immigrants to the United States.

From the late 1960s on, political turmoil in areas of the Muslim world has contributed to Muslim immigration to the United States. In June 1967, Israel decisively defeated its Arab neighbors Egypt, Syria, and Jordan in the Six-Day War. In the process, Israeli forces drove into the West Bank and Gaza Strip areas, where many Palestinians lived. A wave of Palestinian immigration to the West, particularly the United States, followed the war.

In 1979 the secular and westernized regime of Iran's long-time ruler, Shah Mohammed Reza Pahlavi, collapsed. It was replaced by a conservative Islamic government led by the Ayatollah Ruhollah Khomeini. Many Iranians immigrated to the United States to escape the restrictions imposed by Khomeini's hard-line Islamic regime.

In the 1970s and 1980s, several predominantly Muslim countries were torn by violence. In 1971 Bangladesh (East Pakistan) tried to secede from Pakistan and secured independence (with help from

(Inset) The Ayatollah Ruhollah Khomeini, who from exile in Paris inspired opposition to the regime of Iran's ruler, Shah Mohammed Reza Pahlavi. (Main image) Iranian soldiers hold back a crowd of anti-shah demonstrators, 1978. In 1979, after the fall of the shah, Khomeini set up a conservative Islamic government in Iran.

India) after a civil war. In the next 10 years, two Bangladeshi prime ministers were assassinated and the military launched two coups. In Pakistan there was a coup in 1977. In Lebanon a civil war raged from 1975 to 1990. The Soviet Union invaded Afghanistan in late 1979 to prop up a Communist regime, triggering 10 years of fighting; after the Soviets withdrew, various Afghan factions fought one another for power. More recently, there were civil wars in Somalia, Sudan, and Bosnia. All of these conflicts created refugees and contributed to Muslim emigration.

The Middle Eastern Muslims who arrived in the United States after 1965, as well as the South Asians who arrived in the 1970s and 1980s and the Iranians fleeing the Islamic Revolution, were mostly educated and relatively wealthy. Many came to pursue graduate studies and intended to return to their countries when the political turmoil ceased. However, continued political unrest coupled with limited economic opportunities in their home countries caused most of these Muslim students to stay and build families and communities in the United States.

Since the 1990s, more Muslim immigrants have been coming from African nations, including Cameroon, Ghana, Guinea, Kenya, Liberia, Senegal, Sierra Leone, Tanzania, and Uganda. These immigrants are less educated and are poorer than those who arrived when the gates first opened in the 1960s.

Another trend began in the 1980s, corresponding with a rise in Islamism (an ideology that calls for the state's implementation of Islamic law). For the first time, some Muslims began immigrating to the United States in order to transform American society, sometimes through the use of terrorism. At the same time, some Muslims in the United States also began to support Islamist ideology and the transformation of American society into a Muslim nation.

Establishment of Muslim Community Organizations

When Muslims first arrived in the United States, they faced poverty, isolation, and loneliness. Unlike contemporary Christian immigrants, the Muslim arrivals did not have the comfort of being welcomed into existing faith communities. Though they tried to maintain a community and educate the next generation, a lack of institutional support made this difficult and many drifted from religious practice. Furthermore, a lack of accommodations in American public life and the stigma of being marked as different caused many Muslim immigrants to abandon their faith. As the 20th century approached, many Muslims decided to stay in the United States permanently. As the immigrants became more settled, often opening small businesses, they began to assimilate more and drift away from Islamic religious practices. Muslim identity began to be diluted, and intermarriage rose.

Some community structures were formed among the local populations at this time, though there was little institutional support in general—with no formal structures in place until the 20th century. Those that were established focused on creating cultural and social centers for Muslims. The early Muslim immigrants mostly met in homes to pray. Most attempted organizations at this time did not last. For example, one of the oldest Muslim communities founded in America, in Ross, North Dakota, began building a mosque in 1920 but eventually abandoned it when most of the members of the community converted to Christianity.

Organization at the community level picked up after World War I, though the oldest still-existing Muslim organization is Jama'at al-Hajrije, founded by Balkan Muslims in 1906 in Chicago. This was a social-service organization that eventually opened the first Islamic Sunday school. Another early Islamic Center was established in Michigan City, Indiana. It was started by Syrian and Lebanese and eventually attracted more immigrants. One of the earliest mosques established by immigrants from Arab lands was in Cedar Rapids, Iowa. It was begun in 1920 but not completed until 1934. Cedar Rapids was a hub of Muslim life in America in the beginning of the 20th century, and the mosque there is referred to as the "Mother Mosque of America."

Organization on the national level developed after World War II, with the first major organization, the Federation of Islamic Associations, established in 1952 (see Chapter 4). When restrictions on immigration eased in the 1960s, the establishment of many Muslim organizations and mosques flourished. The first Muslim students' association was founded by 1959, but the new wave of Muslims coming to the United States to study was the impetus for the creation of the Muslim Students Association (MSA) in 1963, now one of the largest Muslim groups in the United States. Other organizations, explored in more detail in Chapter 4, were founded during these decades in order to serve the burgeoning Muslim communities. They include the Islamic Circle of North America (1971), the Association of Muslim Social Scientists (1972), United Muslims of America (1982), the Muslim Public Affairs Council (1988), the American Muslim Alliance (1992), the Council on American-Islamic Relations, or CAIR (1994), and the American Muslim Political Coordination Council (1998).

The Islamic Center in Cedar Rapids, Iowa. This building, completed in 1972, replaced the original wooden mosque in Cedar Rapids, which was begun in 1920 and has been called "the Mother Mosque of America."

Demographics of the American Muslim Community

V arious studies and polls offer estimates as to the size of the Muslim community in the United States. On the lower end, a 2001 survey by the City University of New York estimated there to be 1.1 million Muslims in the United States. A 2007 poll conducted by the Pew Research Center, by contrast, calculated the size of the Muslim population in the United States to be around 2.4 million. On the higher end, the Council on American-Islamic Relations (CAIR), a Muslim advocacy group, placed the numbers at between 3.2 and 5.1 million.

What all the reports agree on is that the U.S. Muslim population is continuing to grow from immigration, natural growth, and conversion. A 2007 Pew Survey found that two-thirds of all Muslims in the United States were born abroad. Among the foreign born, most immigrated after 1990. Among the native born, the majority are converts and are African American.

In terms of ethnicity, the largest groups of Muslims in the United States are South Asian, African American, and Arab, with

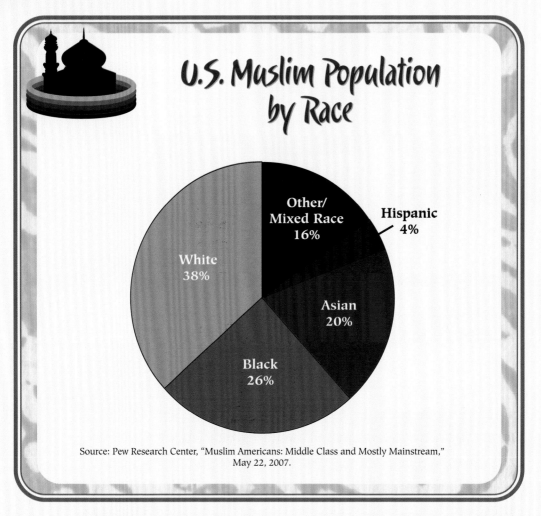

U.S. Muslim Population by Race

Other/Mixed Race 16%

Hispanic 4%

White 38%

Asian 20%

Black 26%

Source: Pew Research Center, "Muslim Americans: Middle Class and Mostly Mainstream," May 22, 2007.

other ethnicities including those from Africa, Europe, Southeast Asia, the Caribbean, Turkey, and Iran. Muslims in the United States come from more than 60 countries. According to the Pew Survey, 38 percent of Muslim respondents consider themselves white, 26 percent black, 20 percent Asian ("Middle Eastern," Iranian, or Arab were not options), 16 percent other/mixed race, and 4 percent Hispanic.

Conversion to Islam

It should also be noted that another segment of the Muslim community in the United States is comprised of converts. While some Americans have converted to Islam individually for reasons of faith or marriage, the Muslim convert community in the United States is comprised mainly of African Americans and grew out of separatist movements of the 20th century that sought to establish a religious identity for African Americans different from that held by whites.

The largest of these groups is the Nation of Islam, founded in 1930 by Wallace Fard Muhammad. This organization is not recognized as part of the mainstream by other Muslim communities, and will not be dealt with in this book.

That said, there are other African-American converts to Islam who identify with Sunni, Shia, and Sufi sects in the United States. There are also trends of Anglo and Latino conversion to Islam. There are between 20,000 and 50,000 Anglo converts to Islam in the United States, and these converts often hold more rigid interpretations of the faith. Conversion among Latino communities is

According to a 2007 Pew Research Center report, 35 percent of American Muslims are converts to Islam. A significant number of these people converted while in prison.

also a noticeable trend in American Islam. This trend began in the 1970s when first-generation Puerto Ricans in New York affiliated with African-American mosques. Latino converts are integrated into established Sunni communities and mosques.

A proportionately high rate of conversions happens among those incarcerated in prisons.

Geographic Distribution

Geographically, Muslims are spread throughout the country, with heavy concentrations in the Northeast, Midwest, southern California, Texas, and Virginia. With the exception of Dearborn, Michigan, Muslims tend to live scattered throughout cities rather than in tight clusters.

The biggest Muslim communities established during the pre–World War I period were in Dearborn; Quincy, Massachusetts; Ross, North Dakota; Chicago; and New York City. The largest number of Muslims who came to the United States settled in the Midwest; California also had a sizeable number, mostly from India. The states with significant Muslim populations at that time included Michigan, Ohio, Indiana, Illinois, Massachusetts, Iowa, Louisiana, New York, and Pennsylvania.

The earliest Muslim arrivals settled in North Dakota. In general, the Midwest was a popular destination for Muslims, particularly those from Syria and Lebanon. It has been claimed that in the early 1900s, Chicago had more Muslims than any other U.S. city. New York City too was home to a sizeable population of Muslim immigrants, being a hub of diverse immigration in general. Muslims from India settled on the West Coast beginning in 1895. These three locations—Chicago, New York, and California— today are home to thousands of Muslims from all over the world.

It is estimated that 20 percent of U.S. Muslims live in California. The region has experienced a significant increase in its Muslim populations since the 1990s. California is now a center for Muslims from all over the globe, particularly those from the Middle East, Iran, South Asia, Afghanistan, and Somalia and other places in Africa. One of the largest Muslim organizations in the world, the Islamic Center of Southern California, is located in Los Angeles.

New York is estimated to have the second-largest concentration of American Muslims, with 16 percent, followed by 8 percent in Illinois, 4 percent in Indiana and New Jersey each, and 3 percent each in Virginia, Texas, Ohio, and Michigan. Dearborn, Michigan, has one of the largest Muslim communities in the United States; it is home to especially large numbers of Lebanese, Palestinian, and Yemeni Muslims, as well as the country's largest

The Islamic Center of America, Dearborn, Michigan. Dearborn, a city of about 92,000, has one of the largest communities of Muslims in the United States.

mosque, the Islamic Center of America, which was rebuilt in 2005 to accommodate more than 3,000 worshippers.

Places of Worship and Study

There are today more than 1,200 mosques spread through the United States, most of which have been built since the 1960s. New York has the most mosques, followed by California, Illinois, New Jersey, Texas, and Michigan. In terms of ethnic identification, African Americans and Indo-Pakistanis have the most mosques, followed by Arabs, though the trend for many mosques is one of non-sectarianism. A 2004 study found that 58 percent of Muslims in the United States view the mosque primarily as a house of worship, while 42 percent view it as a center for activities and learning. However, it is estimated that only 3 to 4 percent of Muslims in the United States attend the mosque at least once a week. A 2000 study found that 70 percent of mosque leaders favored traditionalist or Islamist teachings, while 21 percent adhered to Wahhabism, the strict interpretation favored in Saudi Arabia and often associated with radical Islamist movements internationally.

The affinity toward more strict ideologies can in part be attributed to the fact that many imams (religious leaders) are imported from abroad, particularly from al-Azhar University in Cairo, as well as from Saudi Arabia. These imams do not always speak fluent English and are more resistant to Western values. Their values are not necessarily reflective of the opinions of American Muslims, but they exert influence as the religious leaders.

There are estimated to be about 100 Muslim schools, 500 Sunday Islamic schools, and six Islamic schools of higher learning across the country, though only about 3 percent of Muslim children are said to receive formal Islamic instruction outside of the home (see Chapter 3).

In the classroom at an Islamic school, Abiquiu, New Mexico.

Religious Practice

Religiously, the majority of Muslims in the United States are Sunni. Among the Sunni community, all four schools of jurisprudence are represented. There are also Shia Muslims in the United States. Some estimates say Shia sects comprise one-fifth of Muslims in the United States. Most Shia are from Iran, with a sizeable number from Iraq, as well as some from Lebanon, India, and Pakistan. Shia have particularly strong communities in New York, where they are supported by the al-Kho'i Foundation, and in Dearborn, where the arrival of shaykhs from abroad helped revive the Shia community there.

In smaller communities Sunni and Shia tend to worship in the same mosques, but in larger cities Shia usually have their own places of worship and community centers. In general, mosques tend to follow the practice of the majority ethnicity of their members, but Twelvers from Iran and Muslims from the Indian Subcontinent tend to stay separate since there are many language and cultural differences. It is estimated that 38 percent of Muslims in the United States favor a flexible interpretation of religious texts, while 28 percent prefer the traditional interpretations taught by the classical legal schools. Some Muslims in the United States are members of radical movements, including Salafism, Wahhabism, the Muslim Brotherhood, and Tablighi Jama'at.

In the United States today, there is a tension between recent Muslim immigrants, who tend to favor stringent religious practices, and native-born Muslims, who are more liberal in their

American dating practices can present difficulties for the children of Muslim immigrants, many of whom came from societies with more conservative views of gender relations.

balance between adherence to tradition and integration into American culture. In terms of religious practice, the influence of Western culture manifests itself most in the violation of dietary laws, especially regarding the consumption of alcohol (and to a lesser degree pig and other *haram*, or forbidden, meat). Additionally, young women especially are forced to deal with decisions about Western-style dating versus more traditional methods of finding a partner, such as arranged marriages. In the American context, in certain communities gender segregation has been somewhat relaxed in order to allow young Muslims to socialize within the community. Most Muslims in the United States observe other religious practices such as prayer, fasting during Ramadan, and giving *zakat* (charity).

Muslim Identity

Clearly, the Muslim population of the United States is very diverse, spanning multiple ethnicities and types of religious practice and belief. For this reason, Muslims often feel more of an affinity for their country of origin or ethnic group than toward the larger Muslim community. However, due to internal and external factors, the Muslim community is in a state of transition. Internally, the immigrant generation is maturing and the population of native-born Muslims is growing. Many of the Muslims born in the United States identify more with the rigidities of their religion than do their parents. These second-generation Americans may sympathize with a pan-Islamist, and sometimes militant, revivalist ideology.

The identity of Muslim youth is being shaped in part by religious clerics from the Islamic world who teach these young Muslims how to be devout in a non-Muslim state. Organizations such as the Zaytuna Institute in California are attracting a large youth following. These institutions sponsor intensive religious sessions across the country and are attended by hundreds of Muslim students.

However, a U.S. Institute of Peace report finds that, unlike their coreligionists in Europe and despite strong identification with a Muslim identity, Muslims in the United States do not feel marginalized or unable to participate politically. This is due in part to the fact that in general socioeconomic mobility is achievable in the United States. Muslims have created cultural, religious, civil rights, and political organizations to promote their identity and interests in the United States.

American society, Muslim identity: maintaining traditional Islamic practices can set Muslims apart from the mainstream of U.S. culture.

The "Typical" American Muslim

Seventy-nine percent of Muslims in the United States are between the ages of 16 and 65, and the average Muslim household contains 4.9 people. Muslims work in many sectors, with about 10 percent in engineering and computers, 8 percent in medicine, and 4 percent in finance. It is estimated that Muslims make up 1 percent of the U.S. armed forces. According to a Zogby poll from 2000, average income among Muslims was $53,000, though Arab Muslims earned on average $69,000 while African-American Muslims earned just $32,000. A 2004 Zogby poll found that 59 percent of Muslims in the United States held at least an undergraduate degree. That same poll found that one in three American Muslims earns over $75,000 per year.

Politically, Muslim immigrants tend to vote as a bloc. They voted overwhelmingly for George W. Bush in 2000. However, by

Congressman Keith Ellison and his wife, Kim, ride in a parade. In 2007 Ellison—a Democrat representing Minnesota's Fifth District—became the first Muslim member of the United States Congress.

2004, 85 percent disapproved of Bush, mainly because of his policy toward the Middle East and the wars in Iraq and Afghanistan. In terms of domestic policy, American Muslims tend to be pro-government and socially conservative. A 2007 Pew Research Center study found that 70 percent preferred a big government that spent more and provided more services.

About 10 percent of Muslims in the United States are thought to be associated with Islamist groups. In May 2007, a Pew Research Center study found that 13 percent of Muslims in the United States would justify the use of suicide bombings, albeit "rarely," and that a quarter of young Muslims in the United States support the use of suicide bombing in "some cir-cumstances." Five percent of those surveyed had a favorable or somewhat favorable view of al-Qaeda.

The American Muslim Woman

As with many immigrant and faith groups, family ties are considered of primary importance in the Muslim community, and it often falls to women to maintain family connections. Attitudes toward Muslim women and their place in society differ among different Muslim groups, with differences in particular noted between immigrant Muslim women and native-born ones. In traditional Islamic practice, Muslim women occupy separate space, both literally and figuratively, from Muslim men. Separation of gender figures into Muslim religious practice. That said, since the beginnings of Islam in the United States women have played a role in shaping religious community and family. This participation ranges from being among the founders of various religious communities and mosques to sacrificing for their children in order to raise Muslim Americans who are familiar with their faith while participating in mainstream American society.

A major issue in American Muslim communities revolves around the matter of appropriate dress for women. All agree that the Qur'an prescribes modest dress for both genders, but what this means for women in particular is a matter of debate. The most conservative on this matter tend to be African-American and some Anglo converts,

Although the Qur'an enjoins Muslims to dress modestly, there is no consensus about what precisely that means. For some American Muslims, modesty simply requires women to wear the hijab, or head scarf, when in public. For others, like the woman here, it means covering oneself from head to toe with the burqa.

A clothing store catering to the needs of Muslim women.

who favor clothing that covers the whole body except for the hands and face, including a head covering. Many women opt just for the *hijab* (head scarf). According to Jane Smith, the popularity of the hijab—and more broadly, more conservative dress, including the *jilbab* (robe)—increased after the Israeli victory over the Arabs in 1967, as a way of identifying with Islam and serving as an allegiance to the cause. Today, across the United States there are stores that specialize in Islamic clothing.

There is no consensus among Muslim women in the United States regarding dress. Some happily cover themselves, while others bemoan a pressure to conform to a way of dress that their mothers successfully got rid of as a norm in their home countries, such as Egypt. Some women argue that dressing in an "Islamic" way leads to professional success, since employers respect people they see as pious, yet other women report explicit discrimination in the workplace because of the way they dress and what it is seen to represent.

Americanization of Muslims and Islamization of America

Another issue facing the Muslim community in the United States is the degree of Americanization Muslims face, on the one hand, and the degree of recognition on the other. Thus, education is of paramount importance in this community. Parents worry about influences and pressures in public schools, and thus many promote and support the establishment of private Islamic educational institutions. According to the Council of Islamic Schools in North America (CISNA), there are more than 100 Islamic schools. Muslims are advocating for the implementation of a voucher system that would allow government subsidies to parents to send their children to Islamic school. In 1983, the first Islamic institute of higher education, American Islamic College, was established in Chicago. In 1996, the first Muslim graduate school opened, the School of Islamic and Social Sciences, in Leesburg, Virginia.

In spite of fears of Americanization, American Muslims have made their mark on the American consumer scene, establishing their own stores and products to deal with their needs and ease religious practice in the American context. In addition to clothing stores, there are also specialized travel agents who offer deals to Mecca for the hajj, vendors of educational materials and games, and stores and restaurants specializing in halal food (food ritually fit for consumption according to Islamic law).

Recognition of Muslims and Political Advocacy

One reason, in addition to the obvious need for communal and prayer space, that the Muslim desire to build mosques after World War II grew was out of a belief that the proliferation of visible Islamic structures across the American landscape would legitimize Islam as a faith equal to Christianity on the American scene. In 1957, the Islamic Center opened in Washington, D.C. Built by American Muslims in cooperation with Islamic governments abroad, this structure symbolized the presence of Muslims as part of the fabric of American life.

The recognition of Islam as an American faith has continued to grow. The first president to mention Muslims when listing faiths represented in the United States was Gerald Ford, in 1976.

The Islamic Center in Washington, D.C. "America would fight with her whole strength for your right to have here your own church and worship according to your own conscience," President Dwight D. Eisenhower said at the Islamic Center's dedication on June 28, 1957. "This concept is indeed a part of America, and without that concept we would be something else than what we are."

The first commissioned Islamic chaplain in the U.S. Army, Captain Abdul-Rasheed Muhammad, was appointed in 1993. In addition to serving as a religious adviser for individuals, he has successfully advocated for the accommodation of Muslim needs in the armed forces, included matters related to modest dress, such as wearing a hijab, and diet, such as the provision of halal food.

Recognition has increased because of advocacy efforts at the university level as well. Syracuse University became the first major American university to declare Eid al-Fitr an official school holiday.

In many places in the United States, the growth of the Muslim population has caused public agencies to be sensitive and adapt to their religious needs or claimed requirements. For example, several airports and universities now have special bathrooms where Muslims can perform their ritual ablutions. In response, these institutions have faced criticism for accommodating Muslims at the taxpayers' expense and blurring the line separating religion and state.

Until the 1990s, most American Muslims were reluctant to enter into political life—both because of a refusal to admit that they were staying in the United States for good and, to a lesser extent, because they were heeding religious warnings not to become involved in a non-Muslim political system. Thus, with the growth in the Muslim community in the 1960s, the first

Muslim organizations founded were religious and social centers, often based on ethnicity. Later, educational institutions aimed at preserving cultural identity were established.

Since the 1990s, and especially since the Middle East has become a major focus of U.S. foreign policy, Muslims in the United States have founded numerous organizations devoted to political and social policy. Some of these have been accused of fostering or promoting militant Islam, and individual officials of theirs have been arrested or convicted of involvement with terrorist activities. Others have been sought by the U.S. government as consultants for policy toward Afghanistan and Iraq. Some have worked with U.S. law enforcement agencies to identify intolerance within the Muslim community in the United States; others have rejected such cooperation and tried to restrict investigatory activities.

The growth of the American Muslim population has led some public facilities, such as this airport, to make special accommodations for Muslims.

Muslim Organizations in the United States

There are hundreds of organizations in the United States that cater to the needs of the American Muslim community. Some of these are umbrella organizations. Some focus on political lobbying and ensuring civil rights for Muslims, especially in the wake of anti-Muslim sentiment fostered since the attacks of September 11, 2001. Other groups focus on the cultural needs of particular Muslim groups or on providing an association for coreligionists of certain professions. Some of these groups have been accused of extremist and/or anti-American statements and behavior, though in general the groups provide support to the Muslim community and are accepted organizations on the diverse American scene. This chapter explores a few of the bigger Muslim community, political, religious, and charitable groups.

Islamic Society of North America

One of the largest Muslim organizations in the United States is the Islamic Society of North America (ISNA). Founded by the leaders of the Muslim Students Association, which serves Muslims on campuses across the United States, ISNA is an association of over 300 mostly Sunni immigrant organizations. Its goals include establishing a platform for presenting Islam,

Rushda Majeed, program director of the American Society for Muslim Advancement (ASMA), speaks at a press conference, January 8, 2009. ASMA's stated goals include "strengthening an authentic expression of Islam based on cultural and religious harmony through interfaith collaboration, youth and women's empowerment, and arts and cultural exchange."

supporting Muslim communities, and establishing educational, social, and outreach (including interfaith) programs. Its annual convention is the largest gathering of Muslims in the United States. ISNA's constituency is very diverse. Its diversity has sometimes backfired, with some communities complaining that their needs are not met.

ISNA aims to promote an ideological approach that sees Islam as a total system of life, not a religion confined to the mosque, though it does not subscribe to any particular school of jurisprudence. It focuses on Islam around the world, and does not serve as a reflection of what is going on in the United States. Through its publications, conventions, and speakers, it serves to prevent Muslims from going astray. Some Muslims have accused ISNA of being politically timid and not standing up for Muslims in the wake of September 11. On the other hand, the organization has also been accused of spreading Wahhabist teachings and harboring connections to terrorism.

Islamic Circle of North America

The Islamic Circle of North America (ICNA) was formed by South Asian Muslims as a response to their feeling that ISNA did not adequately address their needs. ICNA's constituents are mostly immigrants or the children of immigrants. They describe themselves as non-ethnic and open to all. ICNA is accused of having a direct connection to a terrorist group, having been identified as the North American front group for Jamaat-i-Islami, a Pakistani Islamist organization based in Kashmir. The other offshoot of ISNA is the Muslim American Society (MAS). Its mission is to promote an understanding of the message of Islam to Muslims and non-Muslims. It focuses on Islamic education and is the parent organization of the Islamic American University. Since September 11, it also serves as a media watchdog. In September

The flag of Pakistan's Jamaat-i-Islami, an Islamist organization some critics allege has close ties with the Islamic Circle of North America.

2004, the Chicago Tribune reported that the MAS was formed by adherents of the Islamist Muslim Brotherhood. The group now claims that it has no connection to the Muslim Brotherhood.

There are a number of Muslim religious/educational organizations, some of which have been accused of being led by teachers with Islamist leanings. The Zaytuna Institute was established in California in 1996 by Hamza Yusuf and Heshem Alalusi. The premise of this institution is that American Muslims need to reconnect with their Islamic heritage. They seek to achieve this goal through classical training in Islamic jurisprudence and Qur'anic studies. The institute's leaders have condemned terrorism and violence in the Middle East and around the world. Another prominent religious organization is the North American Shia Ithna-Asheri Muslim Communities (NASIMCO), the umbrella group for Shia Muslims in North America. The organization publishes books on Shia theology and history and has a Council of Muslim Scholars composed of Shia imams. Another Shia group is the al-Kho'i Foundation, which runs a school. Both groups condemn violence and terrorism against non-combatants.

Political Organizations

There are four main Muslim political organizations that coordinate their activities with each other. The Muslim Public Affairs

Hussein Rashid, professor of Religious Studies at Hofstra University in New York, speaks at a media event to publicize an upcoming conference in Doha, Qatar, sponsored by the group Muslim Leaders of Tomorrow, January 2009.

Council was established in 1988 to effect social change and influence public policy. Its headquarters are in Los Angeles, and it also has offices in Washington, D.C. MPAC's stated aim is to improve the portrayal of Islam and Muslims in the media and in pop culture and to educate the public about Islam.

In 1990, the American Muslim Council (AMC) was formed to increase Muslim political participation and to lobby for Muslim interests in Washington. One of the founders of this organization was Mahmud Abu Saud, a prominent official of the Egypt-based Muslim Brotherhood. The AMC was shut down after September 11 when its founder and former chairman, Abd al-Rahman al-Amudi, was discovered to have illegally accepted money from Libyan officials, which he intended to channel to terrorist groups in Syria. The AMC has since reestablished itself with no connection to its predecessor.

In 1992, the American Muslim Alliance (AMA) was founded in California by Pakistani Muslims with similar aims as the AMC but with a greater focus on grassroots organizing. Finally, the Council of American-Islamic Relations (CAIR), the largest Muslim civil rights and advocacy group, was established in 1994 to campaign against the media for defamation of Muslims and against corporations that discriminate against Muslim employees and customers. There has been a great deal of controversy surrounding CAIR, as the organization has been accused of harassing or slandering critics of radical Islamism and inflating the numbers of anti-Muslim hate crimes, among other things.

These four organizations share their primary foreign policy goal, which is to change the American policy toward the Arab-Israeli conflict. They call for a "need for balance," argue for the reduction of aid to Israel and for companies to divest from Israel, and decry what they view as the disproportionate degree of power held by Jewish lobbies.

Each group has only several thousand members and has been criticized in the Muslim community for focusing too much on foreign policy and the narrow ethnic interests of their founders. MPAC is considered to be the most moderate of the four groups and is the only one that does not accept foreign donations.

At least one organization has been created in response to radical Islamism. The Free Muslims Coalition (FMC) seeks to eliminate support for Islamic extremism by strengthening secular, democratic institutions and supporting reform efforts across the Islamic world. The FMC has publicly denounced terrorism, declared support for the U.S. government's efforts to fight terrorism, and publicly supported the wars in Afghanistan and Iraq. It has also denounced anti-Semitism. Other Muslim organizations have criticized the FMC for aligning itself too closely with the U.S. government.

Similarly, an organization calling itself Muslims Against Terrorism was formed by young Muslim professionals in New York City after September 11. The group spreads an image of Islam as a nonviolent religion, reaching out to other religious institutions such as churches and synagogues, public schools, corporations, and activist groups. It also works with Muslim groups at all levels to stress intolerance toward terrorism.

On the other hand, there are also openly anti-American, jihadist Muslim groups in the United States. These include the U.S. Islamic Thinkers Society.

Charity Organizations

Another category of Muslim groups in the United States includes charity organizations, some of which have ties to radical Islamists abroad. Many of these have been shut down by the U.S. government since September 11 and the passage of the

Patriot Act. In their place, organizations focusing on charity in the United States have been established.

The first group to be shut down after September 11 was the Holyland Foundation for Relief and Development (HLF). HLF was founded in 1987 in Los Angeles as the Occupied Land Fund to raise money for the Palestinian uprising in the West Bank and Gaza Strip. In 1991, HLF changed its name and moved to Richardson, Texas, concurrently setting up additional offices in California, Illinois, and New Jersey. It claimed to be the largest Islamic charity in the United States.

In 1997, it was discovered that the organization had raised over $12 million for Hamas and was promoting that organization. In December 2001, the United States decided to act against HLF because of these connections. In its indictment of HLF, the government claimed that in addition to its ties with Hamas, HLF was "deeply involved with a network of Muslim Brotherhood organizations dedicated to furthering the Islamic fundamentalist agenda espoused by Hamas."

Another indicted charity organization is Global Relief, a group based in Bridgeview, Illinois, that had provided funds to Osama bin Laden and al-Qaeda. It was closed in 2002. So was the al-Haramain Islamic Foundation, an international charity established in 1997 in Ashland, Oregon, and financed by the Saudi government with an international budget of $40 to $60 million. This group was shut down in 2004, and the director, Aqeel Abdel Aziz, was found to have ties to al-Qaeda. In June 2007, a number of Islamist organizations were named as unindicted coconspirators in a federal case in Texas involving fund-raising for terror groups, including Hamas, CAIR, the Muslim Brotherhood, the ISNA, the Islamic Association for Palestine (IAP), the Young Mens' Muslim Society, the Muslim Arab Youth Association, and the North American Islamic Trust. The trial ended in a hung jury in October 2007.

Aided by a U.S. Navy sailor, a member of the humanitarian organization Islamic Relief shrink-wraps a pallet of supplies for Lebanese civilians affected by the 2006 war between Israel and Hezbollah.

Since the closing of these international organizations, American-based and American-focused charities have emerged. One of the chief Muslim charity organizations in the United States is the Inner-City Muslim Action Network (IMAN). The organization sees Islam as part of a larger process of individual empowerment, and through the religion works to improve life in the inner city. Another relief organization is Islamic Relief USA, the American branch of Islamic Relief Worldwide. This group provides aid—for example, to the victims of Hurricane Katrina—without regard to race or religion.

Professional Organizations

There are a variety of Muslim professional organizations in the United States. These include the Islamic Medical Association of North America, the American Muslim Health Professionals, and the National Association of Muslim Lawyers.

Incidents of Islamist Extremism in the United States

While most Muslims in the United States do not support radical Islamism, there is a strong strain of Islamist activism in the United States. Only an estimated 10 percent of Muslims in the United States are believed to be Islamists, with another 5 percent sympathizing with the Islamist cause, and a further 5 percent agreeing with Islamists on certain issues. Yet these are often the most organized and active members of the community, as well as those who control many mosques. Islamists control 80 percent of Muslim institutions, particularly through financing by foreign extremist groups, according to estimates from American foreign policy analyst and conservative commentator Daniel Pipes and the American Jewish Committee.

In 1997, a CIA report found that "approximately one-third of [more than 50] Islamic NGOs [in the United States] support terrorist groups or employ individuals who are suspected of having terrorist connections." These groups are successful because of the huge amounts of funding they receive from abroad. Though many groups deny allegations that they receive foreign aid, many of them have received many millions of dollars from Saudi Arabia and other Gulf countries, which give these countries a big influence over religious instruction.

A 2007 Pew Research Center survey found that 51 percent of Muslim Americans were very concerned about the growth of Islamic extremism around the globe, while 36 percent were very concerned about the possible rise of Islamic extremism in the United States. Still, only 4 in 10 believed that Arabs had carried out the September 11 terrorist attacks, and just 26 percent characterized the U.S.-led "war on terror" as a sincere effort to stop worldwide terrorism. This graffiti image is from New York City.

On the other hand, while trends of extremist Islamist involvement have been noted, some Muslim groups are quick to assert condemnations of terrorism, especially since Muslims have been in the spotlight on this matter since the September 11 attacks. On July 27, 2005, the Fiqh Council of North America, a group composed of 16 mostly Sunni scholars focused on Islamic jurisprudence, issued a fatwa condemning terrorism and religious extremism. "There is no justification in Islam for extremism or terrorism," the fatwa stated. "Targeting civilians' life and property through suicide bombings or any other method of attack is forbidden—and those who commit these barbaric acts are criminals, not martyrs."

The fatwa was supported by 200 Muslim organizations and mosques (out of 1,200 mosques and hundreds of organizations). Some critics of the fatwa note that it does not specifically name Osama bin Laden and al-Qaeda, or other groups, as terrorists.

Pre-September 11 Incidents

While only a small percentage of Muslims in the United States have been in some way involved with terrorist activity against the United States, there have been a number of attacks, the chronology of which begins before the events of September 11, 2001. It is important to note that according to a Pew survey in 2007, 61 percent of Muslims in the United States express concern over the rise of Islamic extremism in the United States.

Before the September 11 attacks, the most notorious and deadliest terror attack by Muslim extremists inside the United States occurred in February 1993. It also targeted the World Trade Center, but with a truck bomb instead of aircraft. The 1993 World Trade Center bombing, which killed six people and injured more than 1,000, was inspired by Omar Abd al-Rahman, a radical cleric from Egypt who came to the United States in an effort to fund-raise and organize for the international jihadist group Maktab al-Khidmat. Also in 1993, a plot to simultaneously bomb the United Nations and the Lincoln and Holland tunnels in New York City was uncovered.

Ramzi Yousef, mastermind of the 1993 World Trade Center bombing. Captured in Pakistan in 1995, Yousef was extradited to the United States, where he was tried, convicted, and sentenced to life imprisonment without parole.

Post-September 11 Incidents

There have been a number of incidents in the United States or involving American

On July 4, 2002, Hesham Mohamed Hadayet—an Egyptian immigrant to the United States—opened fired at the ticket counter of El Al, the Israeli national airline, at Los Angeles International Airport. Hadayet killed two people before he was fatally shot by a security guard.

Muslims since September 2001. For example, in 2002 an Egyptian opened fire at the El Al airline counter at Los Angeles International Airport and killed three people. In 2006 a Pakistani immigrant attacked the Jewish Federation of Greater Seattle, killing one and injuring six. These events of course do not implicate the Muslim community as a whole, nor do they amount to the type of anti-U.S. sentiment expressed by the events of September 11. However, they do show the problematic relationship between Muslims residing in the United States and the Jewish community there, as well as a resort to violence to protest American policy toward the Middle East.

Several Muslim individuals have also been arrested for their involvement in terrorist activity. In 2002, John Walker Lindh, an

American convert to Islam, pled guilty to serving with the Taliban, which violated U.S. economic sanctions against Afghanistan. Six immigrants from Yemen living in Lackawanna, New York, were convicted of giving support to al-Qaeda and training in an al-Qaeda camp. In 2007, Jose Padilla, along with two other Muslims—a computer programmer and a school administrator from Detroit—was convicted of conspiracy to support terrorism and raising money and providing support for terrorism. Padilla's case is interesting, however. While he did indeed engage in illegal activities associated with terrorism, his case also is an example of government disregard for rights and of the trend of dissemination of false information (regarding the production of a "dirty bomb") despite the lack of an actual charge.

In 2003, Iyman Faris was convicted of providing resources to al-Qaeda, providing the terrorist group with information about possible targets, and plotting to destroy the Brooklyn Bridge. In 2005, Ahmad Omar Abu Ali was convicted of providing support to al-Qaeda, conspiring to assassinate the president of the United States, and planning to commit air piracy. Also in 2005, Ali al-Tamimi was convicted of recruiting Muslims in the United States to fight against U.S. troops in Afghanistan. In 2006,

John Walker Lindh in the custody of U.S. forces in Afghanistan, December 2001. Lindh, a Californian who was raised a Catholic, converted to Islam at age 16. Later, he traveled to Yemen and Pakistan, eventually ending up in Afghanistan as a 20-year-old soldier in the army of that country's ruling regime, the Taliban. Shortly after the U.S. invasion of Afghanistan—which was undertaken in response to the terrorist attacks of September 11, 2001—Lindh was captured by Afghan allies of the United States. In 2002 he pled guilty to violating U.S. economic sanctions against the Taliban and was sentenced to 20 years in prison.

Derrick Shareef was charged with attempting to explode hand grenades in garbage cans in a mall in Illinois.

Institutional Connections to Terror

CAIR in particular has been accused of having links to foreign Islamic terrorism. The radical Islamist involvements CAIR has are well known. The organization was founded by members of the Holyland Foundation for Relief and Development (HLF) and the Islamic Association of Palestine (IAP), also known as the American Muslim Society, which were later proven to have connections to Hamas. While the leadership denies this and has offered a blanket condemnation of the use of terror, it has not condemned any specific groups. While CAIR has been successful in its goals of preventing discrimination against Muslims and helping to get Muslims elected to public office and has been accepted by the mainstream media as well as by Democratic and Republican politicians, the organization was nonetheless declared an unindicted coconspirator in a federal terror-funding trial in June 2007.

At times, CAIR officials have publicly endorsed Islamist terrorism. According to Judith Colp Rubin, in 1992, Siraj Wahaj, a CAIR board member, said in a speech that if Muslims in America, "[w]ere united and strong, we'd elect our own emir [leader] and give allegiance to him. . . . [T]ake my word [for it], if 6–8 million Muslims unite in America, the country will come to us." Later, Rubin reports, in February 1995, Wahaj was named as a possible coconspirator in the 1993 bombing of the World Trade Center. In 1994, CAIR founding member and executive Nihad Awad stated publicly that he supported Hamas, and more than a decade later, it was discovered that his name appeared on a list of members of the Palestine Committee, an organization created to help Hamas financially and politically.

Ibrahim Hooper, the organization's communications director, defended the financial aid Saudi Arabia gives to families of Palestinian suicide bombers.

Furthermore, several people affiliated with CAIR were arrested for terrorist-related activities while working at the organization, including Randall "Ismail" Todd Royer, a CAIR communications specialist and civil rights coordinator, who, among 10 other Muslims, was involved in a Northern Virginia–based organization that planned to engage in terror against the United States. He was sentenced to 20 years in jail. Rabid Haddad, a CAIR fund-raiser, had also been executive director of the Global Relief Foundation, which the United States found had raised money for al-Qaeda; Haddad was subsequently deported.

Attitudes Toward the United States and Islam

Since the events of September 11, 2001, Muslims have risen in the American public's consciousness, often in a negative light. However, post–September 11 attitudes are not new. Unfortunately, America has a history of anti-Muslim prejudices and discrimination, dating back to the first instances of Muslim immigration in the 19th century. Even then, the image of "the Arab" has been of a character with a hook nose and shifty eyes. In more recent years, this caricature has evolved into the image of a terrorist, and for many Americans, the terms *Muslim* and *terrorist* are erroneously interchangeable. Nonetheless, this image has been reinforced through cartoons in newspapers as well as through popular Hollywood films.

Since the arrival of Muslims on American soil, there have been complaints of discrimination—for example, regarding zoning regulations that allegedly restricted the building of mosques.

This poster for Buffalo Bill's Wild West Show, printed around 1899, featured Arab horsemen billed as "the Real Sons of the Soudan." Historically, many Americans viewed Muslims as exotic or alien. More recently, some Americans have viewed Muslims as dangerous.

This controversy has not subsided, though the locations and cases in question change.

Anti-Terror Policy

Mainstream American reactions to the types of terrorist activities mentioned in the previous chapter, in addition to the more prominent attacks of September 11, have caused Muslims in the United States to report that in recent years they have often felt judged and discriminated against in mainstream American society. This is also due to the Patriot Act, a piece of legislation passed in October 2001; it eased restrictions on intelligence gathering and has been used to deny visas to foreigners and to deport residents. According to a 2007 Pew Research Center study, 54 percent of Muslims in the United States feel that U.S. anti-terrorism policy and activity single out Muslims. The problem, of course, is that Islamist terrorists are Muslims and often

President George W. Bush speaks about the Patriot Act, Charleston, South Carolina, February 5, 2004.

use Muslim groups or mosques to recruit, propagandize, raise funds, and organize activities.

Muslims in the United States believe the most serious issues confronting their community are discrimination, being viewed as potential terrorists, and mainstream America's ignorance about Islam as a religion. A study by Cornell University in December 2004 found that 27 percent of Americans supported the idea of requiring all Muslim Americans to register their home address with the government. Around 29 percent thought undercover agents should infiltrate Muslim organizations.

Discrimination Against Muslims

Muslims have been the victims of discrimination and hate crimes, including vandalism against mosques, harassment against women wearing the hijab, and discrimination in the workplace, though the numbers of such actions are matters of debate. Claims of Muslims being racially profiled and humiliated in searches at airports and other public places have been reported. Fifty-three percent of American Muslims reported that it was harder to be a Muslim in the United States after September 11, 2001. Continued suspicion against Muslims can be seen in the events surrounding the 2008 presidential elections. Many Americans had no problem publicly admitting that they would not vote for Barack Obama because he was a Muslim. Though Obama is not actually a Muslim, the fact that people thought that would be a reason to discriminate against him is telling. Nonetheless, Obama was in fact elected, overcoming all sorts of prejudices, not just anti-Muslim ones.

A 2007 Pew Research Center study found that most Muslims in the United States are assimilated and happy. However, nearly half (47 percent) said they consider themselves Muslims first and Americans second (a lower percentage than Muslims in

Europe though). Only 43 percent agreed that Muslims coming to the United States should adopt American customs.

Only 40 percent believe that Arabs were responsible for the September 11 attacks, with 28 percent skeptical, despite public claims of responsibility by al-Qaeda. Among this 28 percent, a

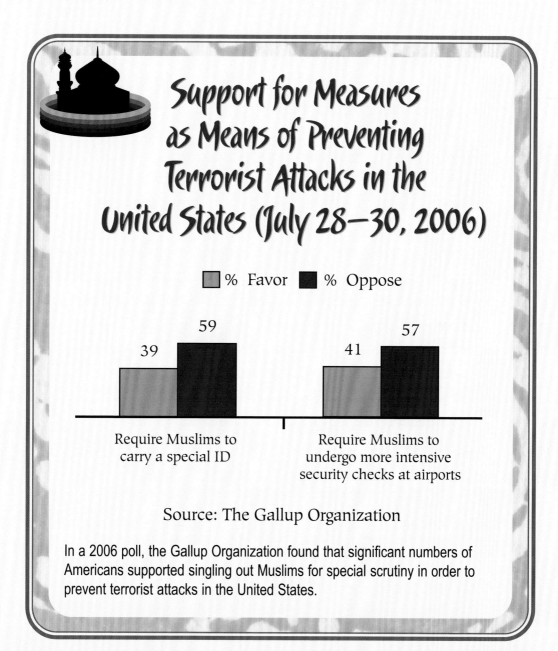

Support for Measures as Means of Preventing Terrorist Attacks in the United States (July 28–30, 2006)

☐ % Favor ■ % Oppose

Require Muslims to carry a special ID: 39, 59

Require Muslims to undergo more intensive security checks at airports: 41, 57

Source: The Gallup Organization

In a 2006 poll, the Gallup Organization found that significant numbers of Americans supported singling out Muslims for special scrutiny in order to prevent terrorist attacks in the United States.

quarter believes that the real culprit was the U.S. government and the Bush administration. Only 26 percent believe that the war on terror represents a sincere effort to wipe out terrorism. Thirty-five percent agreed with the U.S. decision for military action in Afghanistan, while only 12 percent concurred regarding the U.S. attack on Iraq.

Attitudes Toward Muslims

For their part, non-Muslim Americans do not have particularly positive views toward Muslims in the country. According to a 2007 *Newsweek* poll, 46 percent of Americans believe that there are too many Muslims in the United States, and 32 percent believe that American Muslims are less loyal to the United States than to Islam (which is actually a lower percentage than what Muslims reported about themselves). A 2003 Pew poll found that over the previous year Americans' unfavorable attitude toward Islam increased by 1 percentage point, to 34 percent. By 2005, this view was shared by 36 percent of those surveyed, while 55 percent expressed a favorable opinion, an increase from the 45 percent reported in March 2001, before the September 11 attacks. A CBS poll in 2006 reported that only 19 percent of Americans viewed Islam as a faith favorably, though 55 percent of Americans did have a favorable opinion of Muslims.

By July 2005, only 36 percent of Americans believed that Islam was more likely than other religions to encourage violence, down from 44 percent two years earlier. Sixty-three percent of Americans, according to a 2007 *Newsweek* poll, believed that American Muslims do not condone violence, though 28 percent believe the Qur'an condones violence, and 41 percent think Islamic culture glorifies suicide.

Hostility against Muslims in the United States is lower than it is in Canada and European countries.

The coming years will be critical as Muslims situate themselves within the fabric of American society.

It is clear that there are differing attitudes both within and about the Muslim community in the United States. At this stage, only a small percentage of Muslims in the United States actively identify with extremist groups or ideologies, but the effects of this Islamism are felt in the United States, as they are around the world, both through attacks and through the enormous influence these organizations wield over civic, political, and religious Muslim institutions in the United States.

For their part, mainstream Muslims in the United States have felt marginalized and discriminated against, though they also believe they can build happy and integrated lives for themselves in the United States. The coming years will determine toward which direction the Muslim community in the United States will head as Muslims continue to attempt to situate themselves within the fabric of American society.

Chronology

1600s–1800s: Muslims from West Africa arrive in America as slaves. Most lose their connection to Islam in the New World.

Ca. 1870: First wave of voluntary Muslim immigration to the United States begins. It is composed mostly of Arab men from the Ottoman Empire seeking to earn money and return home.

1906: Jama'at al-Hajrije, the oldest still-existing Muslim organization in the United States, is established by Balkan Muslims in Chicago.

1920: One of the first mosques in the United States is built by Arab immigrants in Cedar Rapids, Iowa.

1924: Congress passes a law restricting immigration; it slows the flow of Muslim arrivals to the United States.

1952: The Federation of Islamic Associations, the first major national Muslim organization in the United States, is established.

1953: The Nationality Act is passed; it places a quota on immigrants from each country based on populations in the United States at the end of the 19th century, which means that Muslim immigration is still restricted.

1957: The Islamic Center opens in Washington, D.C. It is built by American Muslims in cooperation with Islamic governments abroad and symbolizes the presence of Muslims as part of the fabric of American life.

1963: The Muslim Students Association is founded.

1965: The quota system for immigration is repealed, and Muslim immigration begins to rise.

1976: For the first time, a U.S. president lists Islam as an American faith.

1983: The American Islamic College, the first Islamic institute of higher education in the United States, is established in Chicago.

1993: On February 26, Islamist radicals detonate a truck bomb in a parking garage under the World Trade Center in New York City.

2001: On September 11, terrorists sponsored by the group al-Qaeda hijack four commercial jets, crashing two into the Twin Towers of the World Trade Center and one into the Pentagon outside Washington, D.C.; the fourth plane crashes into a field in western Pennsylvania after a struggle between passengers and the hijackers.

2005: The Fiqh Council of North America issues a fatwa condemning terrorism and religious extremism.

2007: In January, Keith Ellison is sworn in to the U.S. House of Representatives, becoming the first Muslim member of Congress. The Council on American-Islamic Relations (CAIR) is declared an unindicted coconspirator in a federal terrorism-funding trial.

Glossary

fatwa—a non-binding religious opinion given by a Muslim scholar based on Islamic law.

fiqh—rulings derived from the Qur'an that deal mostly with ritual and social practice (literally, the word *fiqh* means "jurisprudence").

hajj—the pilgrimage to Mecca, which all Muslims are obligated to undertake at least once in their lifetime, if they are physically and financially able.

halal—a designation denoting actions or objects that are permissible according to Muslim law, often in reference to food.

hijab—the head covering worn by some Muslim women.

Muslim Brotherhood—a transnational radical movement whose goal is to create states based on Islamic law.

Qur'an—Islam's holy scriptures, which are a key source of Islamic law and practice.

Wahhabism—conservative, fundamentalist Islamic ideology.

Further Reading

Ba-Yunus, Ilyas and Kassim Kone, *Muslims in the United States* (Westport, CT: Greenwood Press, 2006).

Curtis, Edward E., *The Columbia Sourcebook of Muslims in the United States* (New York: Columbia University Press, 2008).

Haddad, Yvonne Yazbeck, ed., *The Muslims of America* (New York: Oxford University Press, 1991).

Hasan, Asma Gull, *American Muslims: New Generation* (New York: Continuum, 2002).

"Muslim Americans: Middle Class and Mostly Mainstream," Pew Research Center, May 22, 2007. http://pewresearch,org/assets/pdf/muslim-americans.pdf.

Pipes, Daniel, *Militant Islam Reaches America* (New York: W.W. Norton & Co., 2003).

Smith, Jane I., *Islam in America* (New York: Columbia University Press, 1999).

Zogby, John, "American Muslim Poll." (Washington, DC: *Project MAPS: Muslims in the American Public Square*, Zogby International, 2001).

Internet Resources

http://www.meforum.org/docs/cat/13

> This site provides links to articles about Muslims in the contemporary United States.

http://theamericanmuslim.org/

> This site is a forum for Muslims interested in pluralism. It is a valuable resource for information about Muslims in the United States.

http://www.usip.org/pubs/specialreports/sr159.html

> The site offers a report titled "The Diversity of Muslims in the United States: Views as Americans," United States Institute of Peace Special Report, No. 159 (Washington, DC: United States Institute of Peace, February 2006).

Index

Numbers in **bold italics** refer to captions.